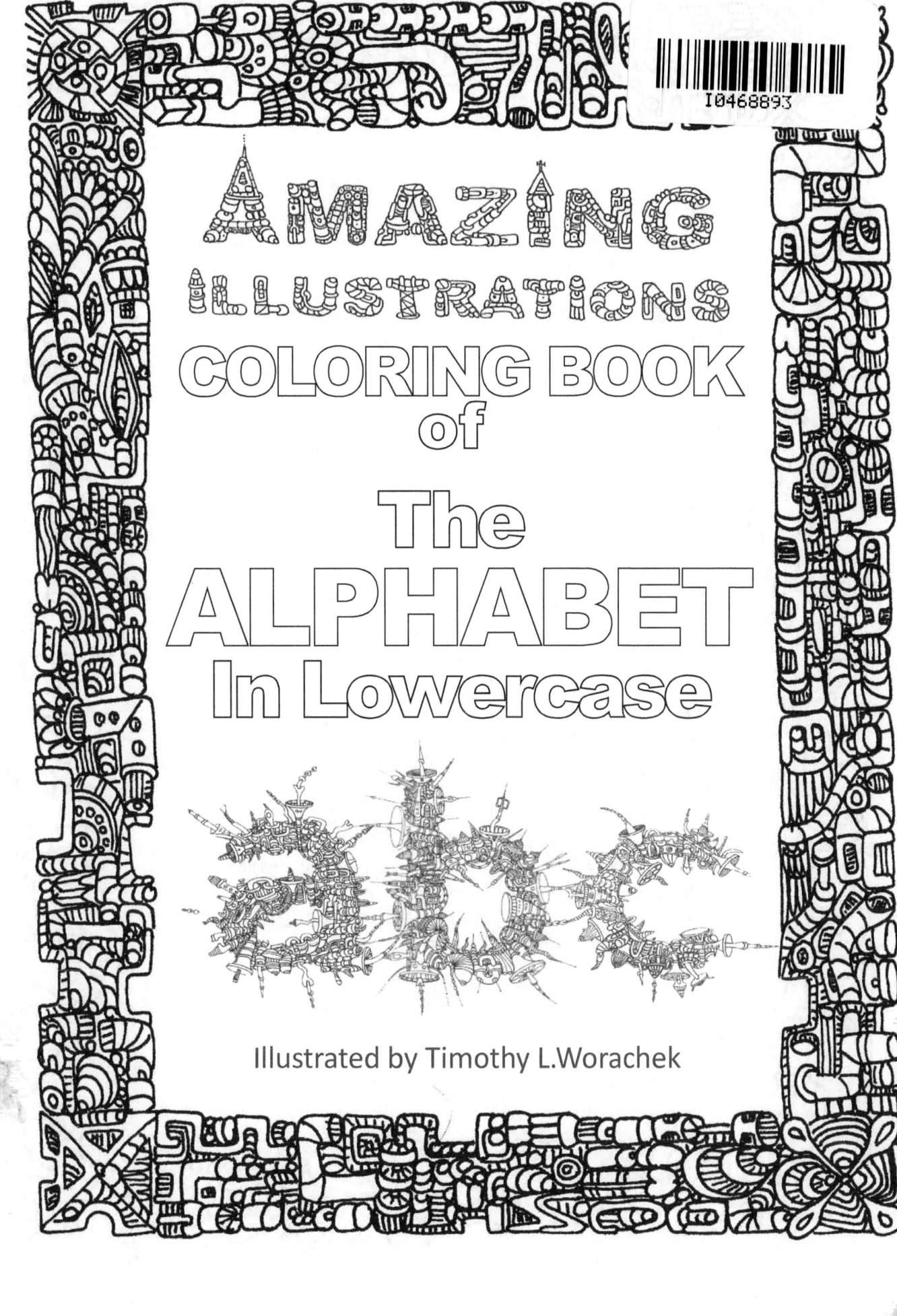

AMAZING ILLUSTRATIONS
COLORING BOOK
of
The
ALPHABET
In Lowercase

Illustrated by Timothy L.Worachek

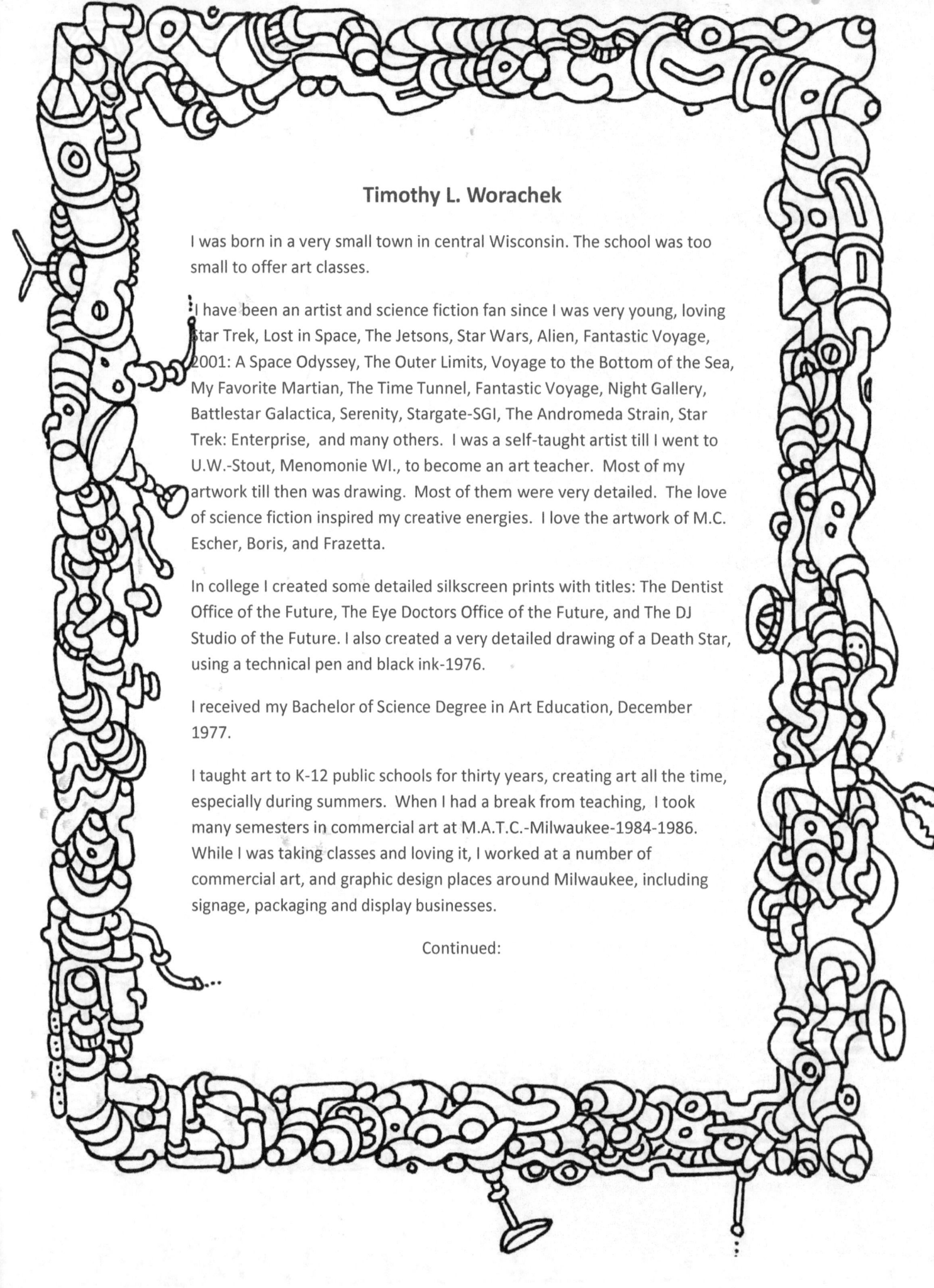

Timothy L. Worachek

I was born in a very small town in central Wisconsin. The school was too small to offer art classes.

I have been an artist and science fiction fan since I was very young, loving Star Trek, Lost in Space, The Jetsons, Star Wars, Alien, Fantastic Voyage, 2001: A Space Odyssey, The Outer Limits, Voyage to the Bottom of the Sea, My Favorite Martian, The Time Tunnel, Fantastic Voyage, Night Gallery, Battlestar Galactica, Serenity, Stargate-SGI, The Andromeda Strain, Star Trek: Enterprise, and many others. I was a self-taught artist till I went to U.W.-Stout, Menomonie WI., to become an art teacher. Most of my artwork till then was drawing. Most of them were very detailed. The love of science fiction inspired my creative energies. I love the artwork of M.C. Escher, Boris, and Frazetta.

In college I created some detailed silkscreen prints with titles: The Dentist Office of the Future, The Eye Doctors Office of the Future, and The DJ Studio of the Future. I also created a very detailed drawing of a Death Star, using a technical pen and black ink-1976.

I received my Bachelor of Science Degree in Art Education, December 1977.

I taught art to K-12 public schools for thirty years, creating art all the time, especially during summers. When I had a break from teaching, I took many semesters in commercial art at M.A.T.C.-Milwaukee-1984-1986. While I was taking classes and loving it, I worked at a number of commercial art, and graphic design places around Milwaukee, including signage, packaging and display businesses.

Continued:

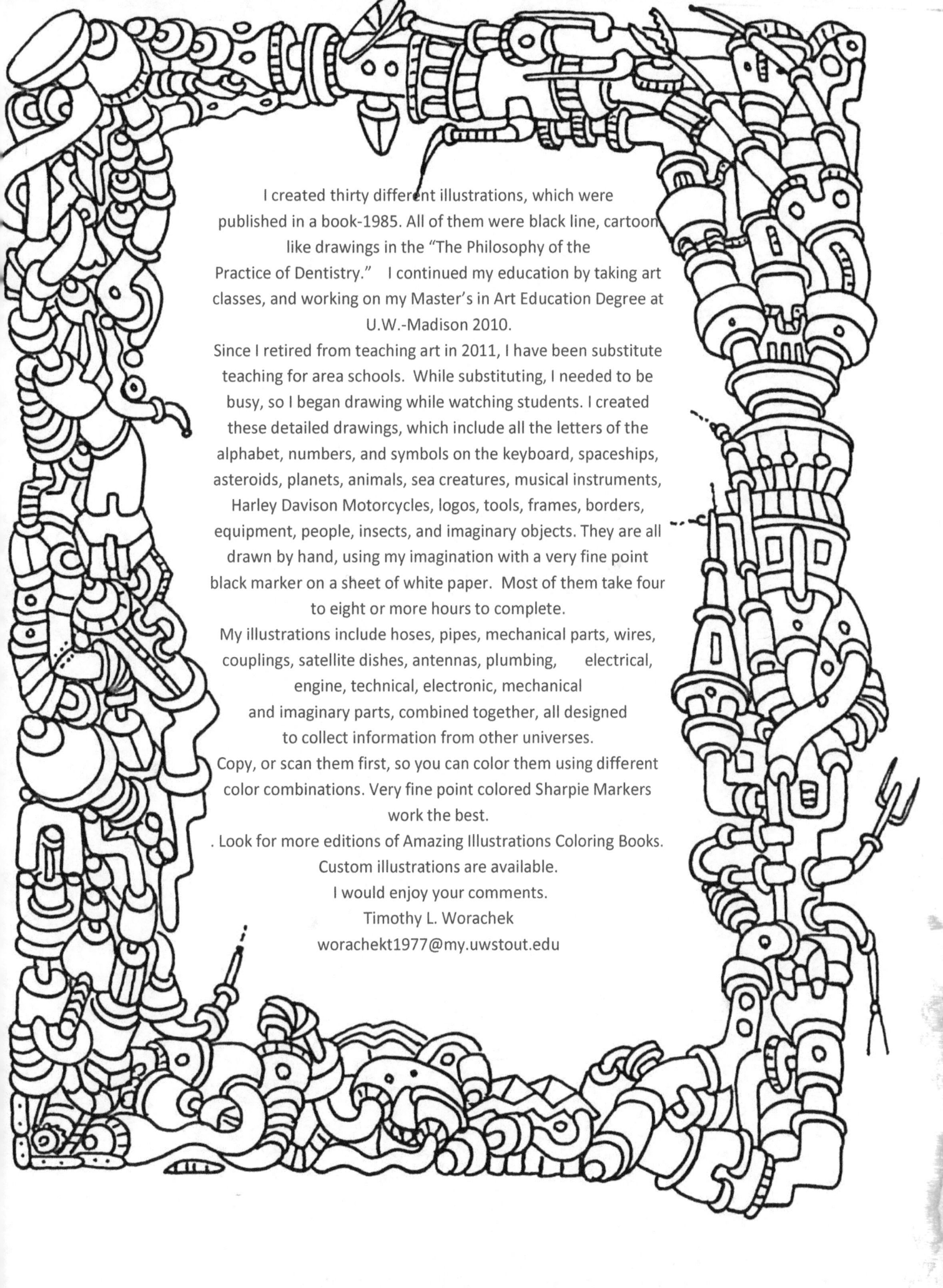

I created thirty different illustrations, which were
published in a book-1985. All of them were black line, cartoon
like drawings in the "The Philosophy of the
Practice of Dentistry."   I continued my education by taking art
classes, and working on my Master's in Art Education Degree at
U.W.-Madison 2010.

Since I retired from teaching art in 2011, I have been substitute
teaching for area schools. While substituting, I needed to be
busy, so I began drawing while watching students. I created
these detailed drawings, which include all the letters of the
alphabet, numbers, and symbols on the keyboard, spaceships,
asteroids, planets, animals, sea creatures, musical instruments,
Harley Davison Motorcycles, logos, tools, frames, borders,
equipment, people, insects, and imaginary objects. They are all
drawn by hand, using my imagination with a very fine point
black marker on a sheet of white paper. Most of them take four
to eight or more hours to complete.

My illustrations include hoses, pipes, mechanical parts, wires,
couplings, satellite dishes, antennas, plumbing,   electrical,
engine, technical, electronic, mechanical
and imaginary parts, combined together, all designed
to collect information from other universes.

Copy, or scan them first, so you can color them using different
color combinations. Very fine point colored Sharpie Markers
work the best.

. Look for more editions of Amazing Illustrations Coloring Books.
Custom illustrations are available.
I would enjoy your comments.
Timothy L. Worachek
worachekt1977@my.uwstout.edu

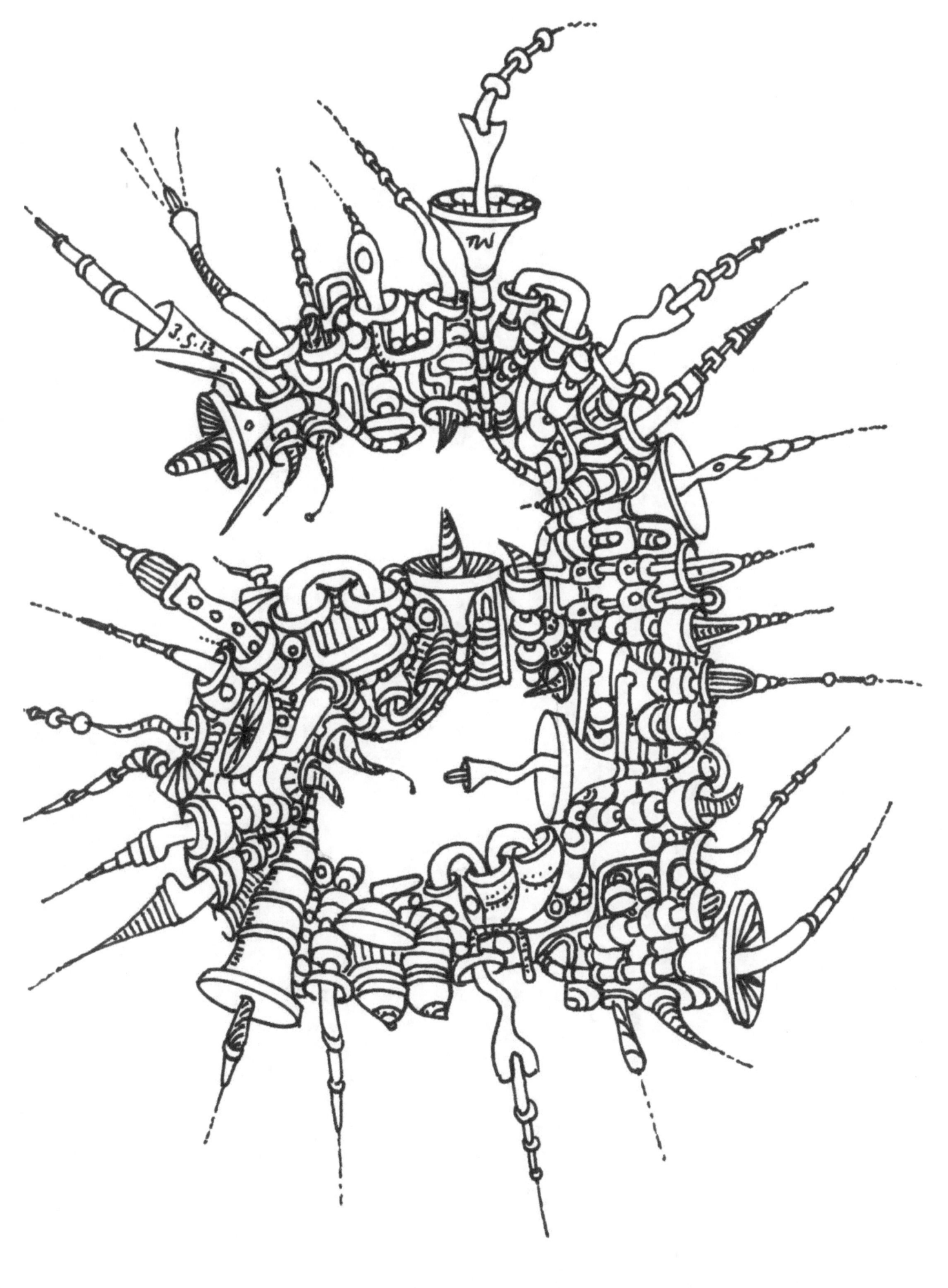

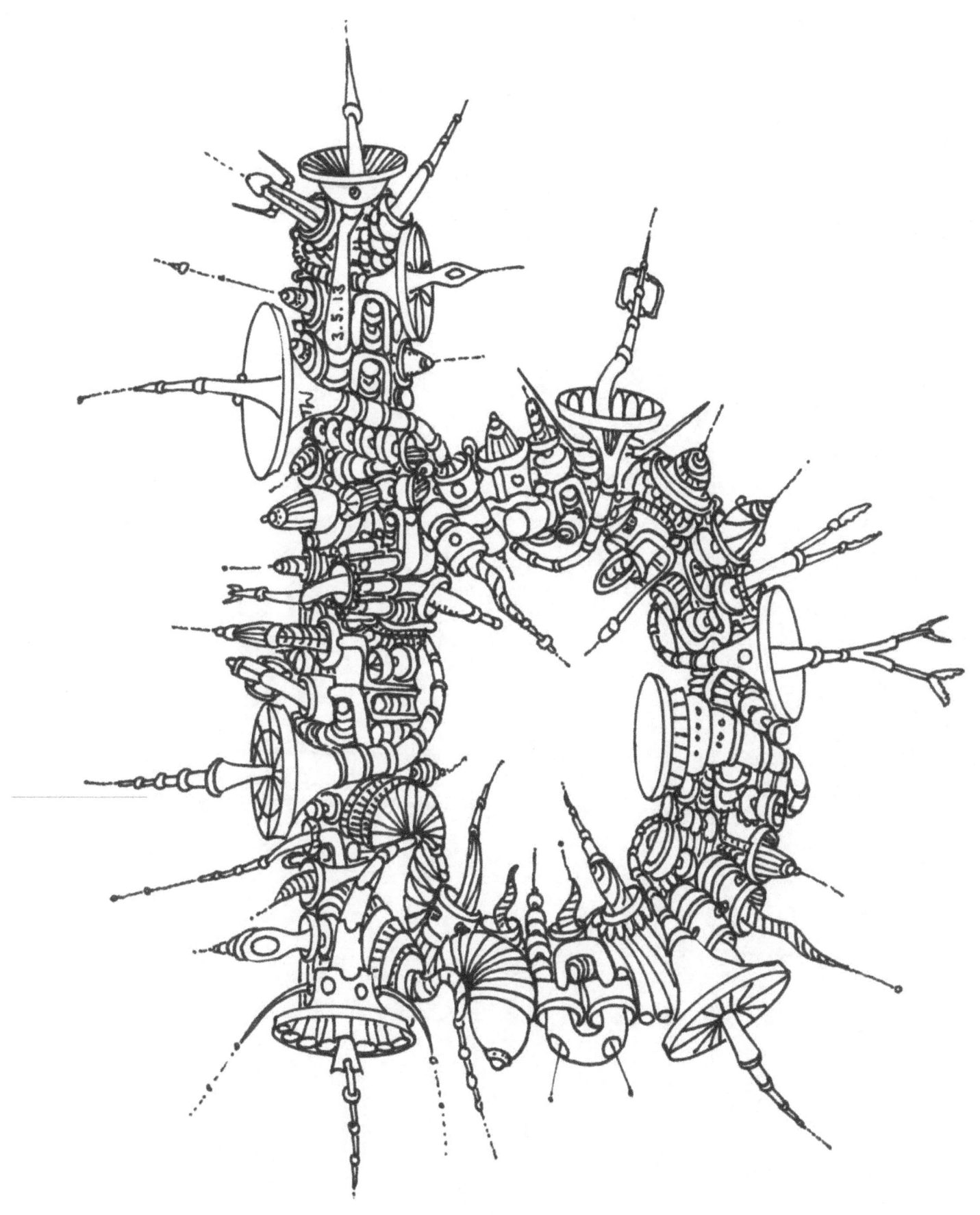

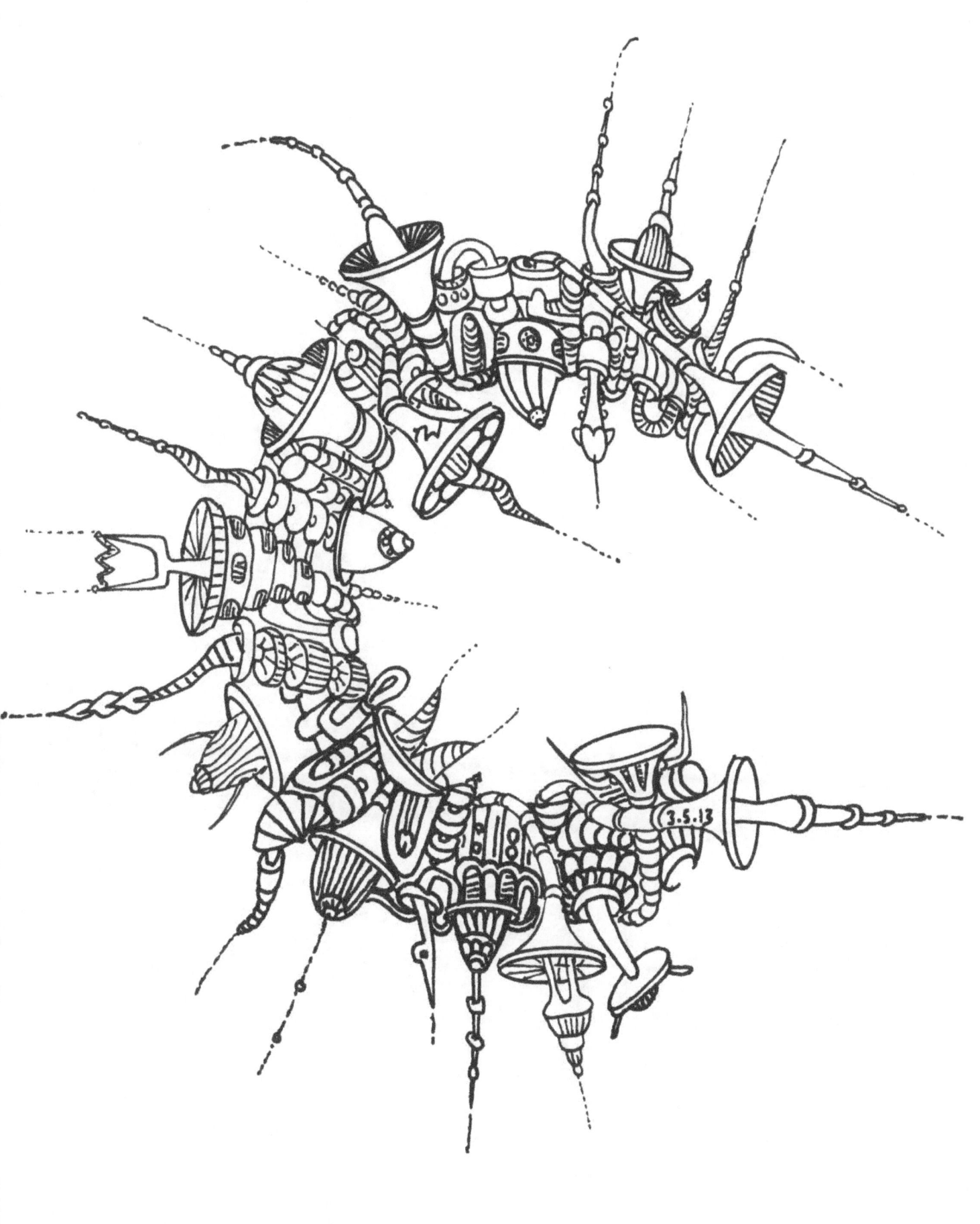

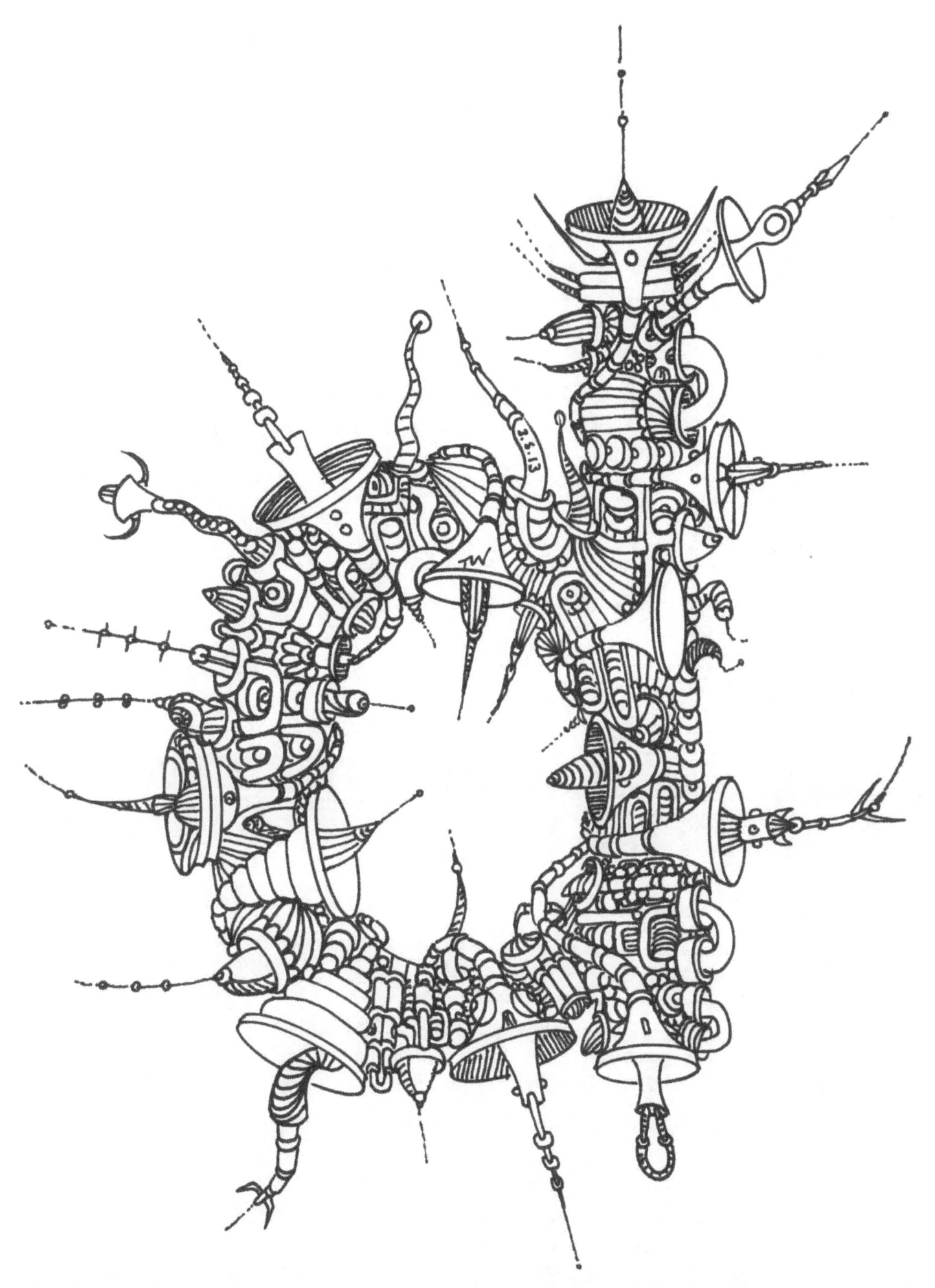

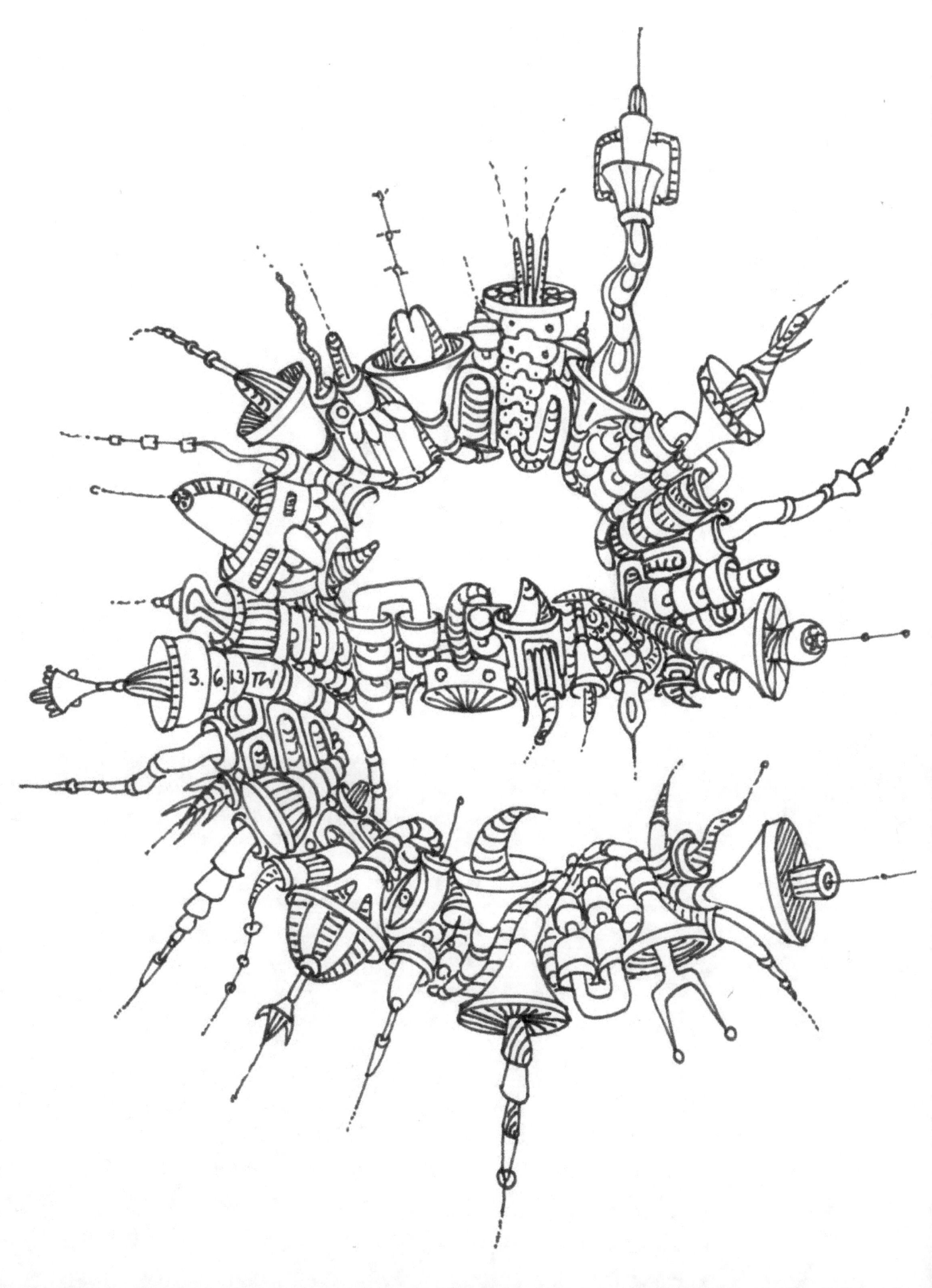

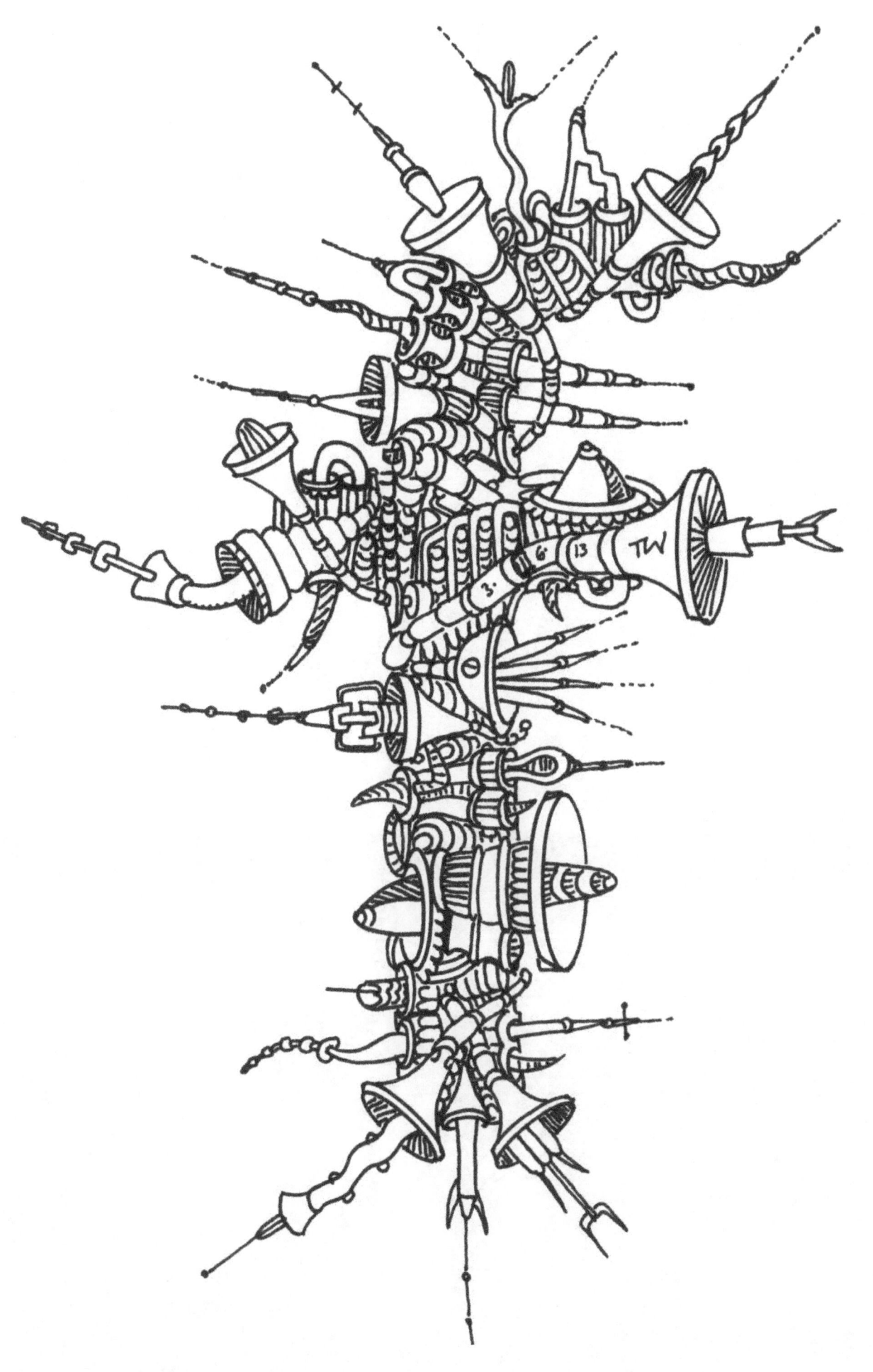

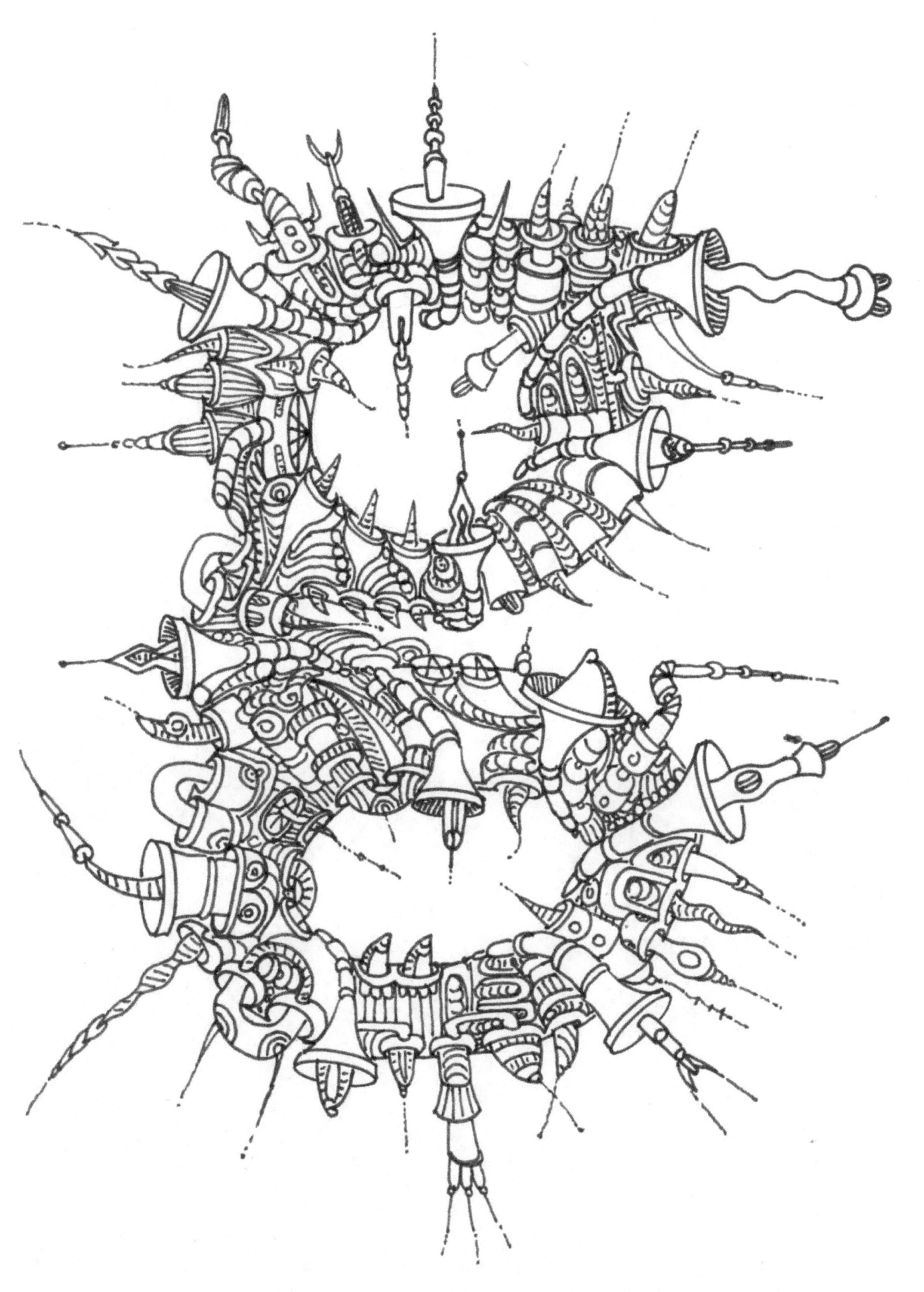

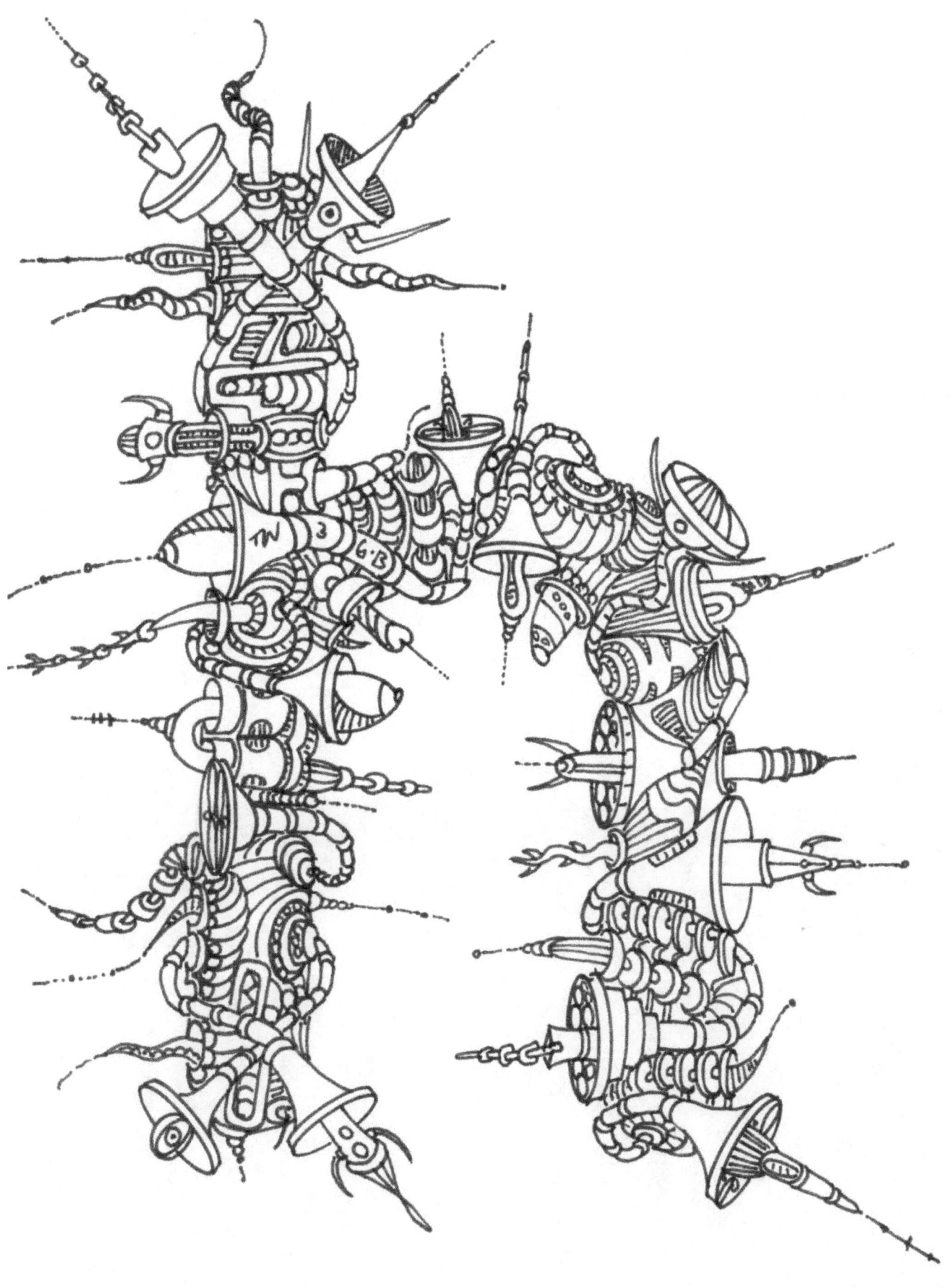

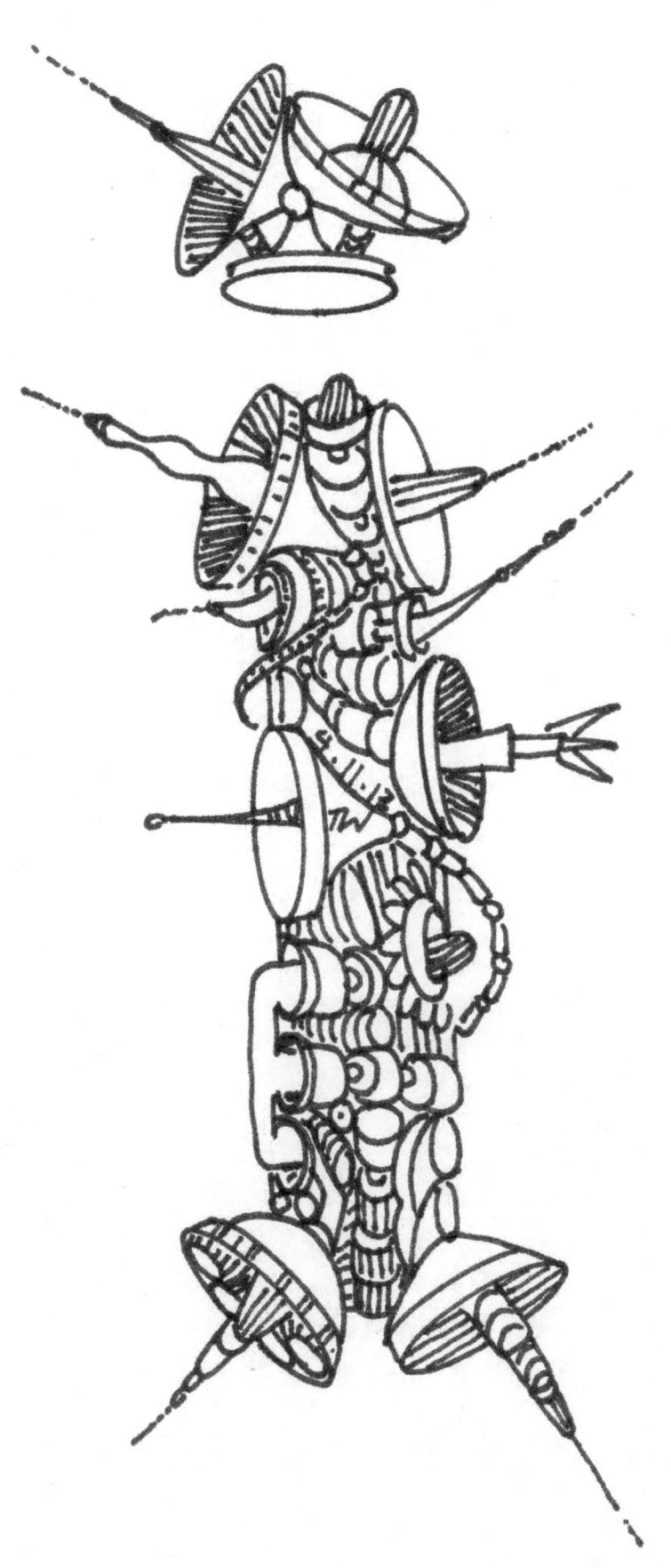

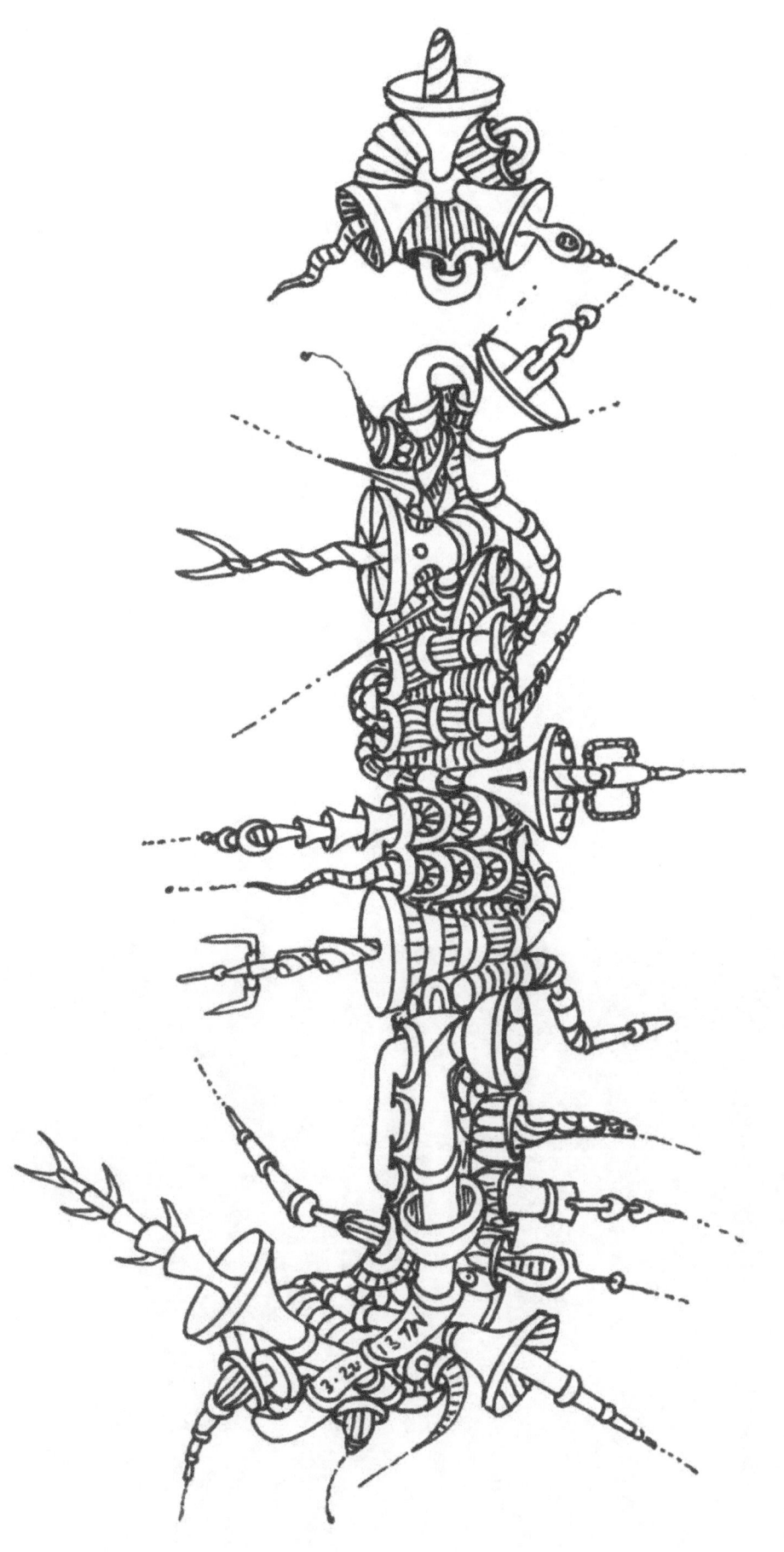

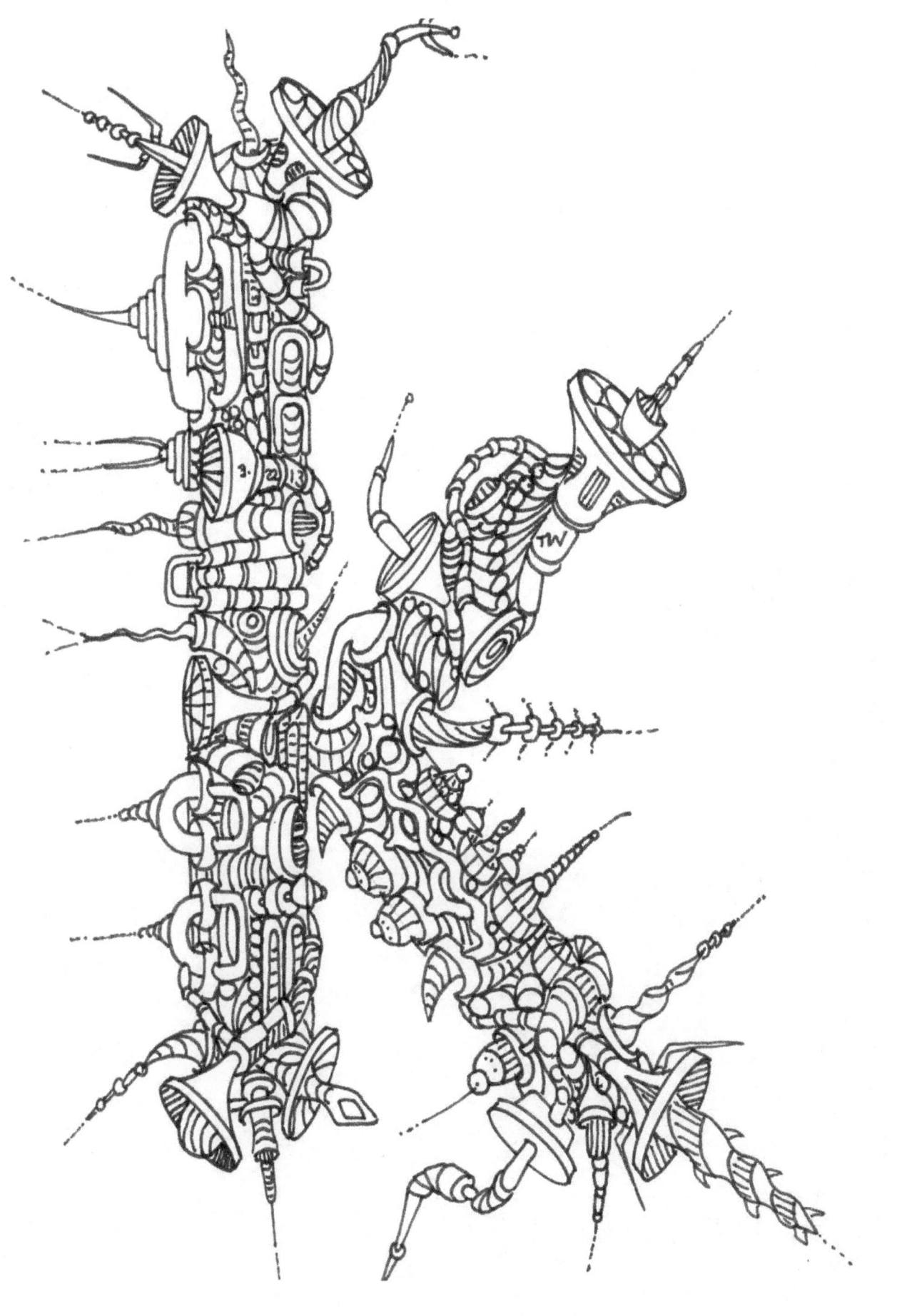

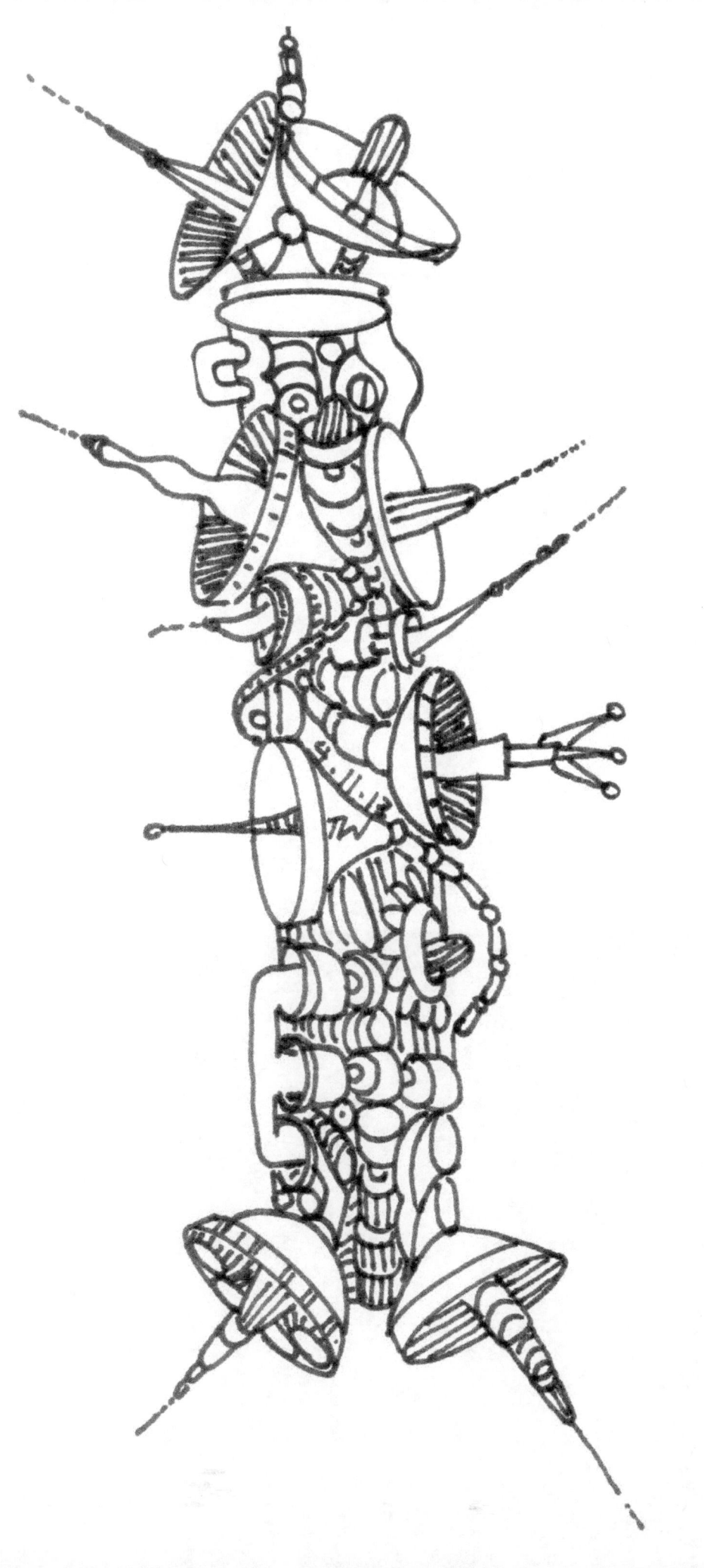

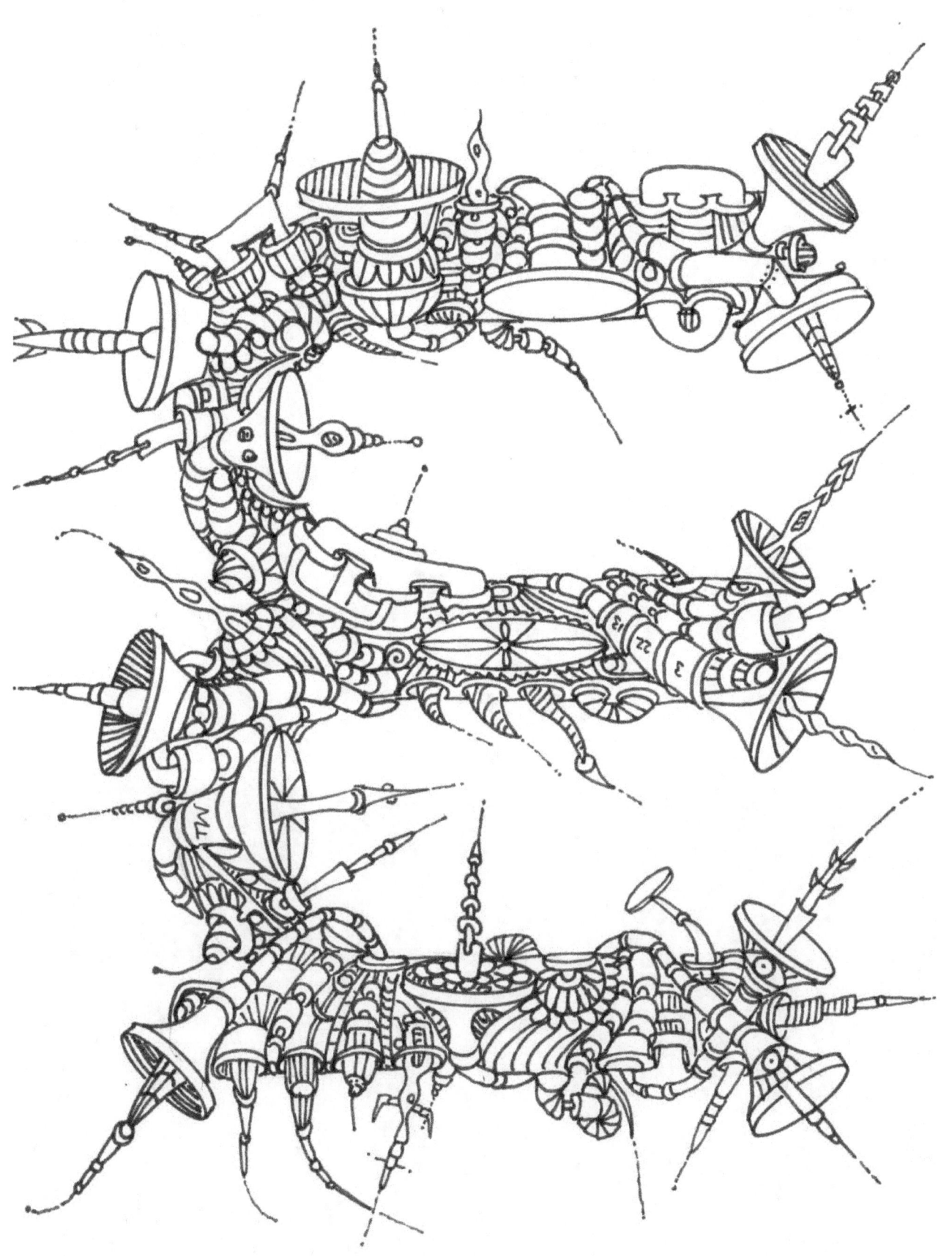

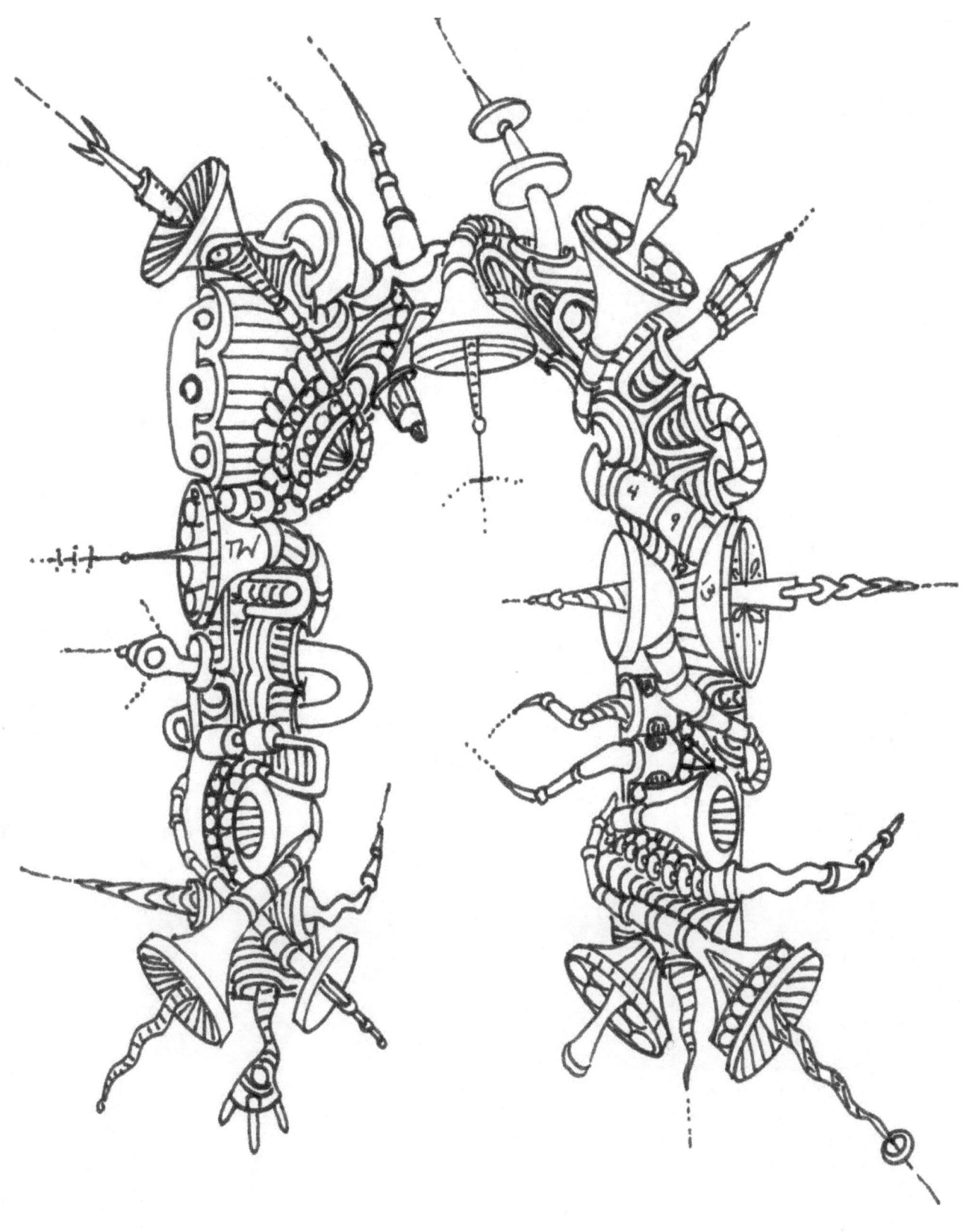

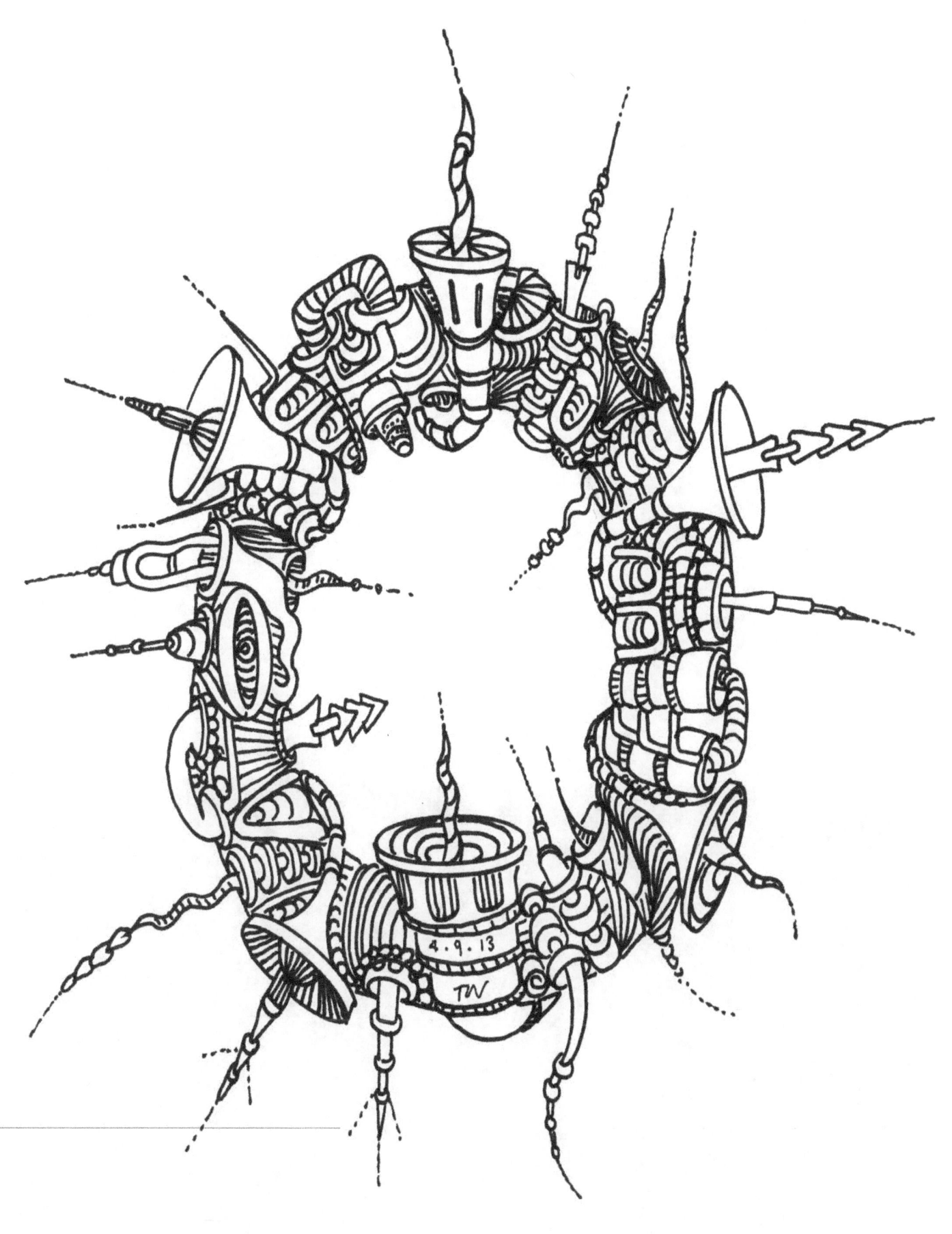

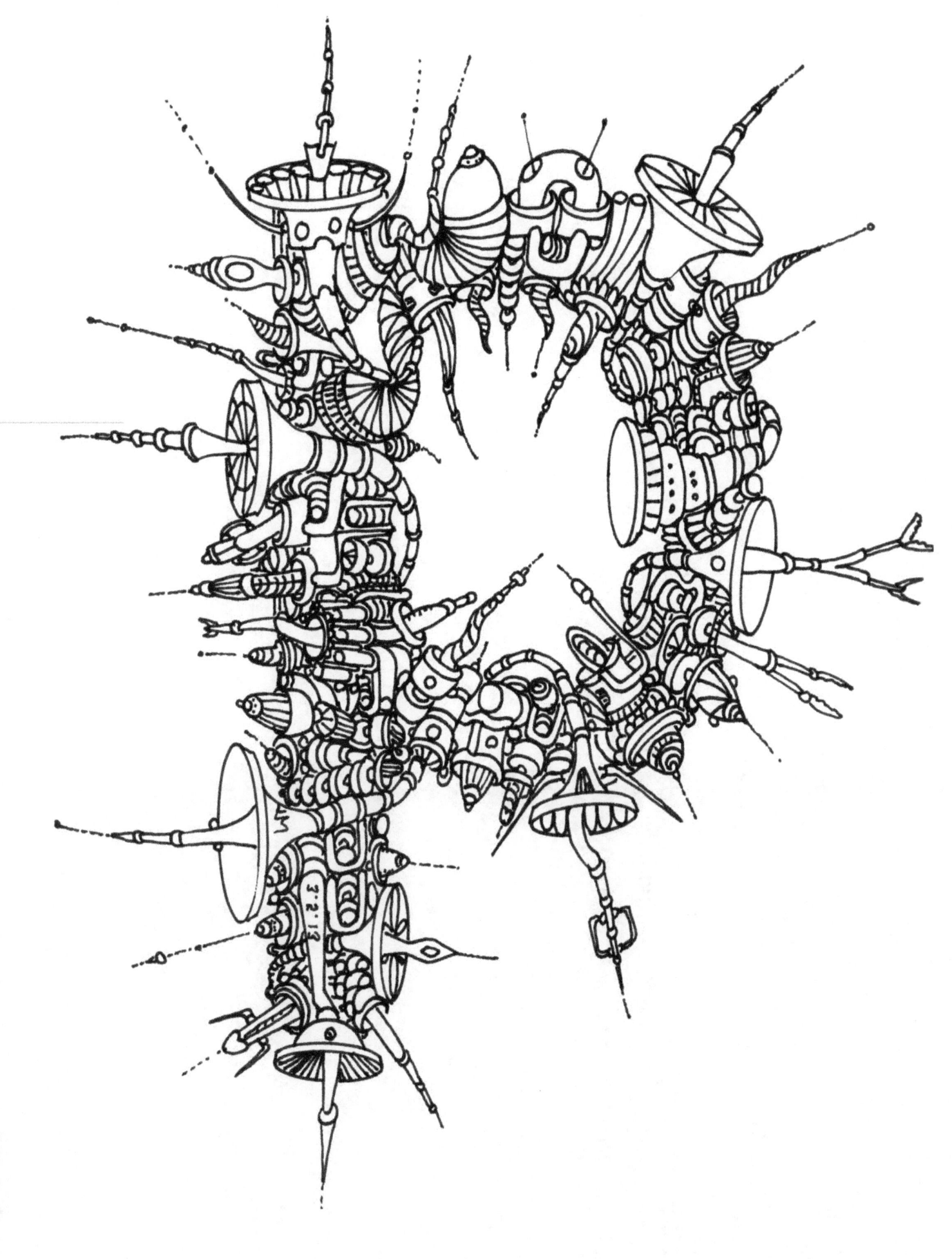

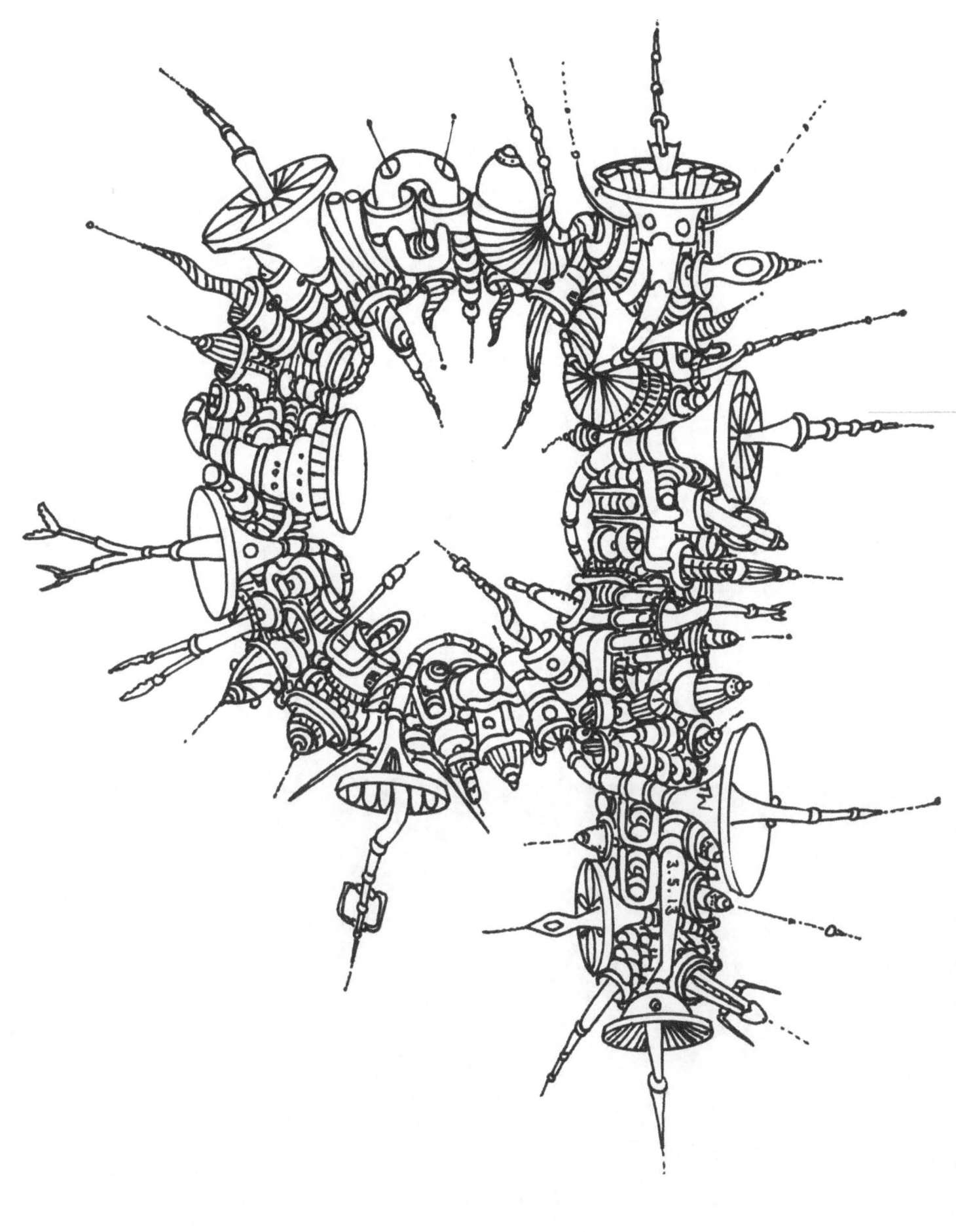

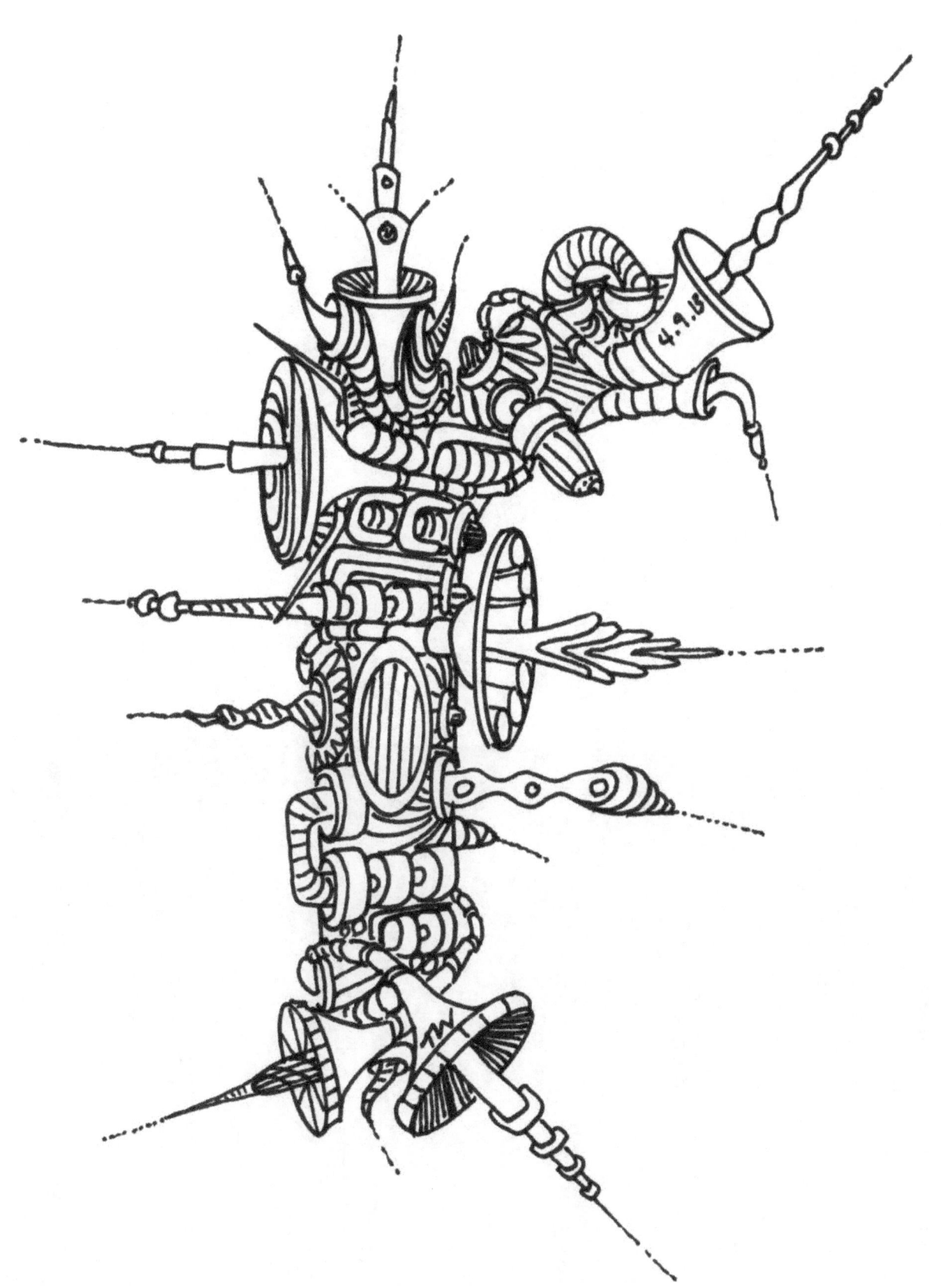

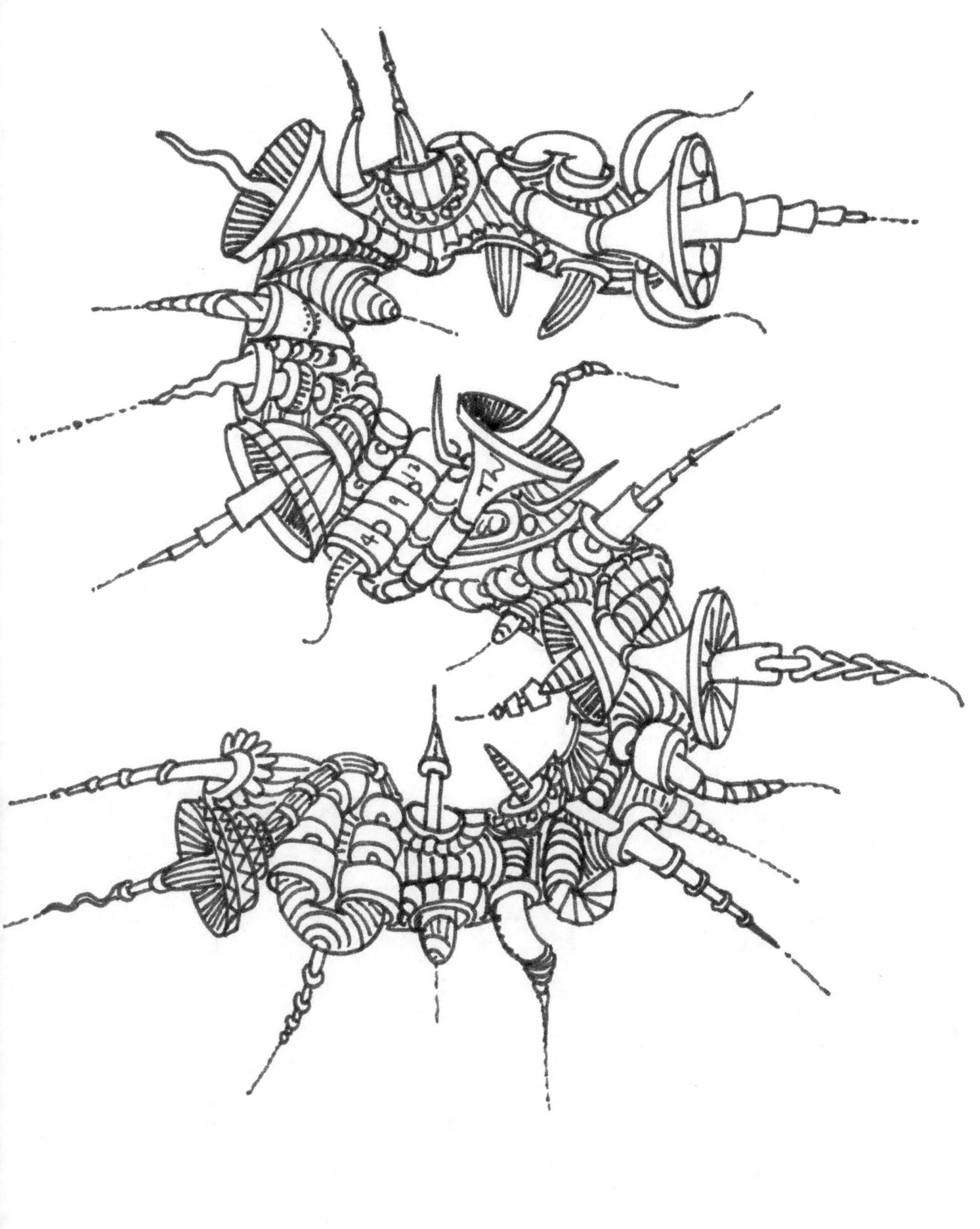

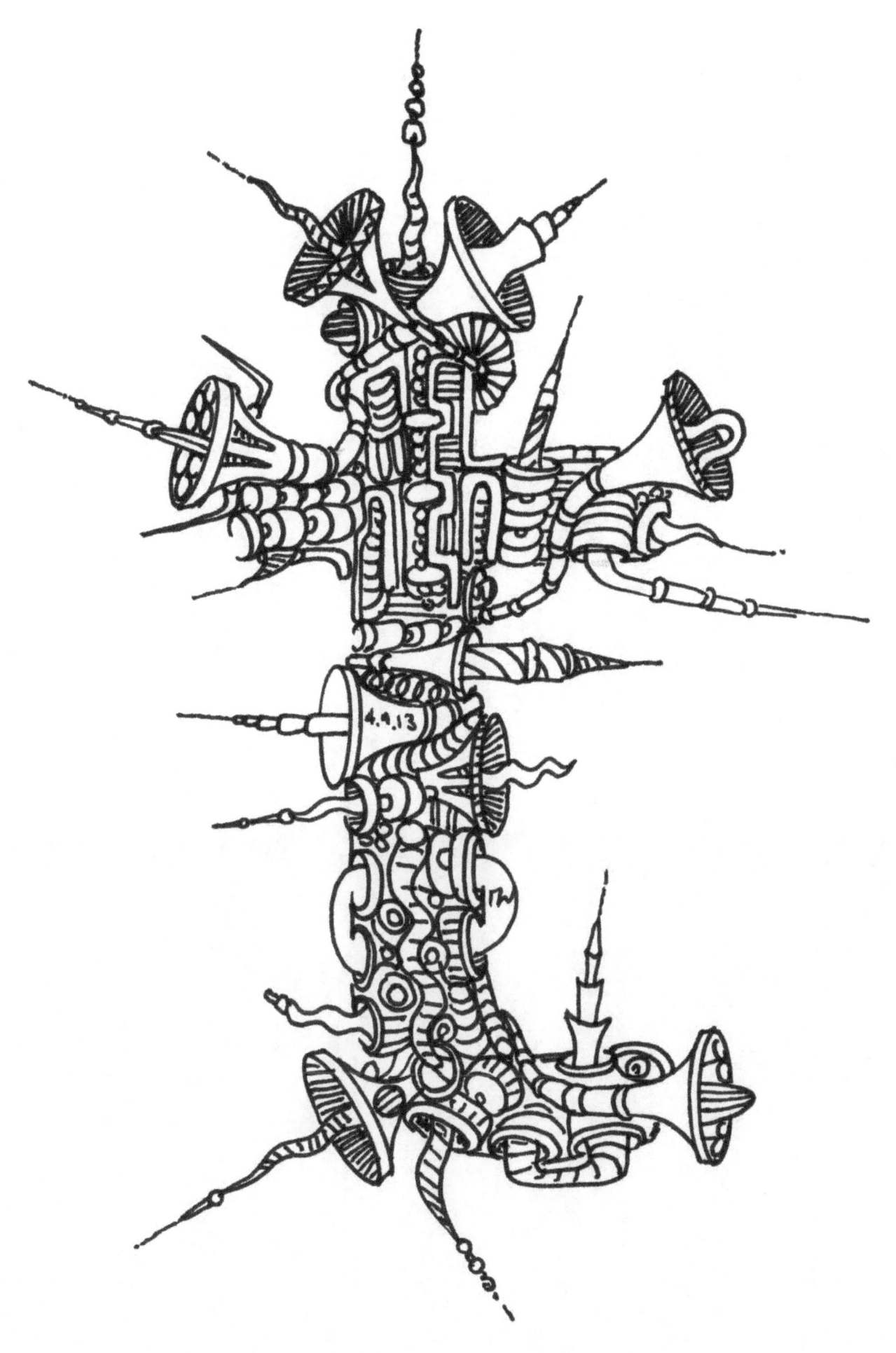

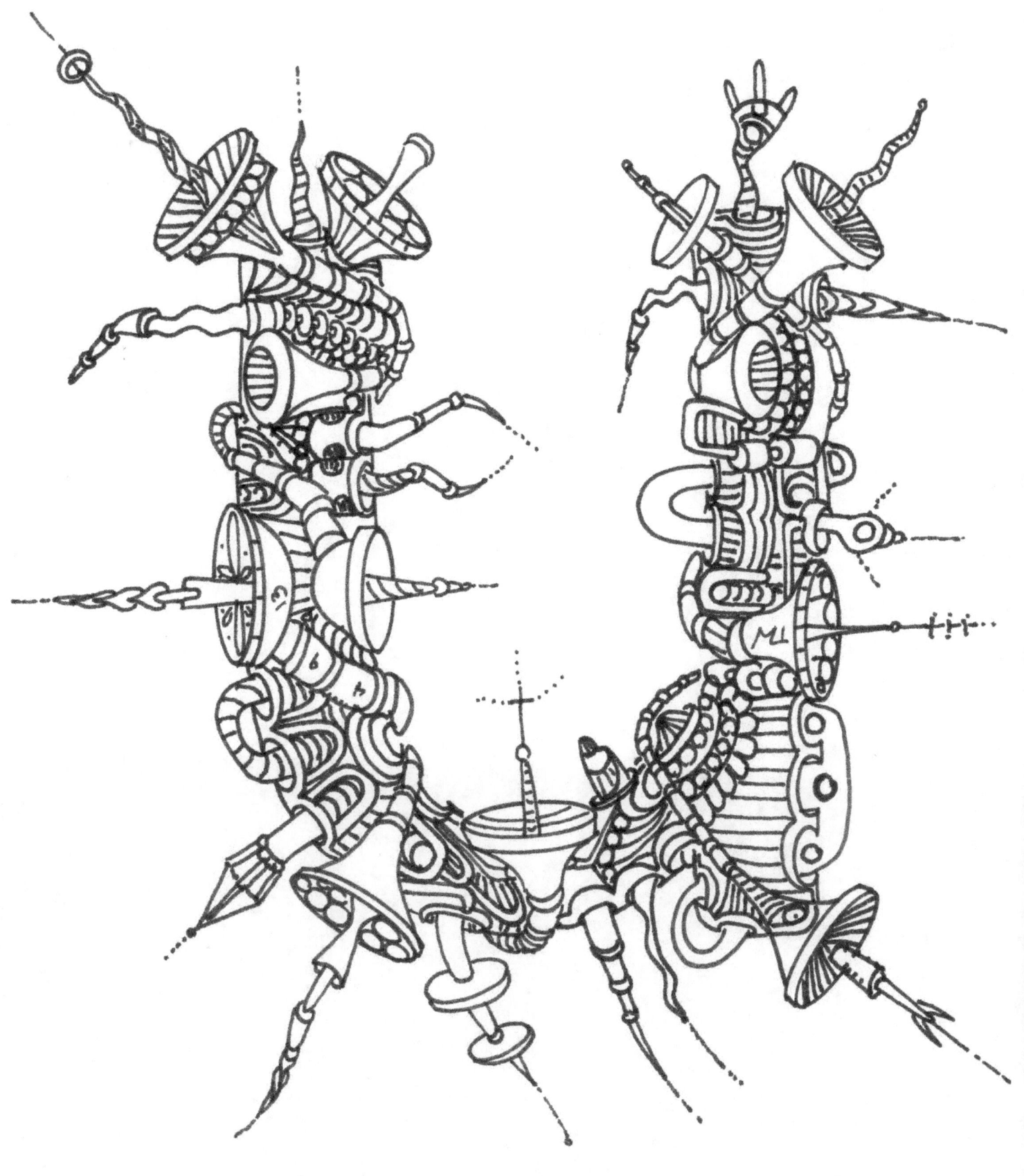

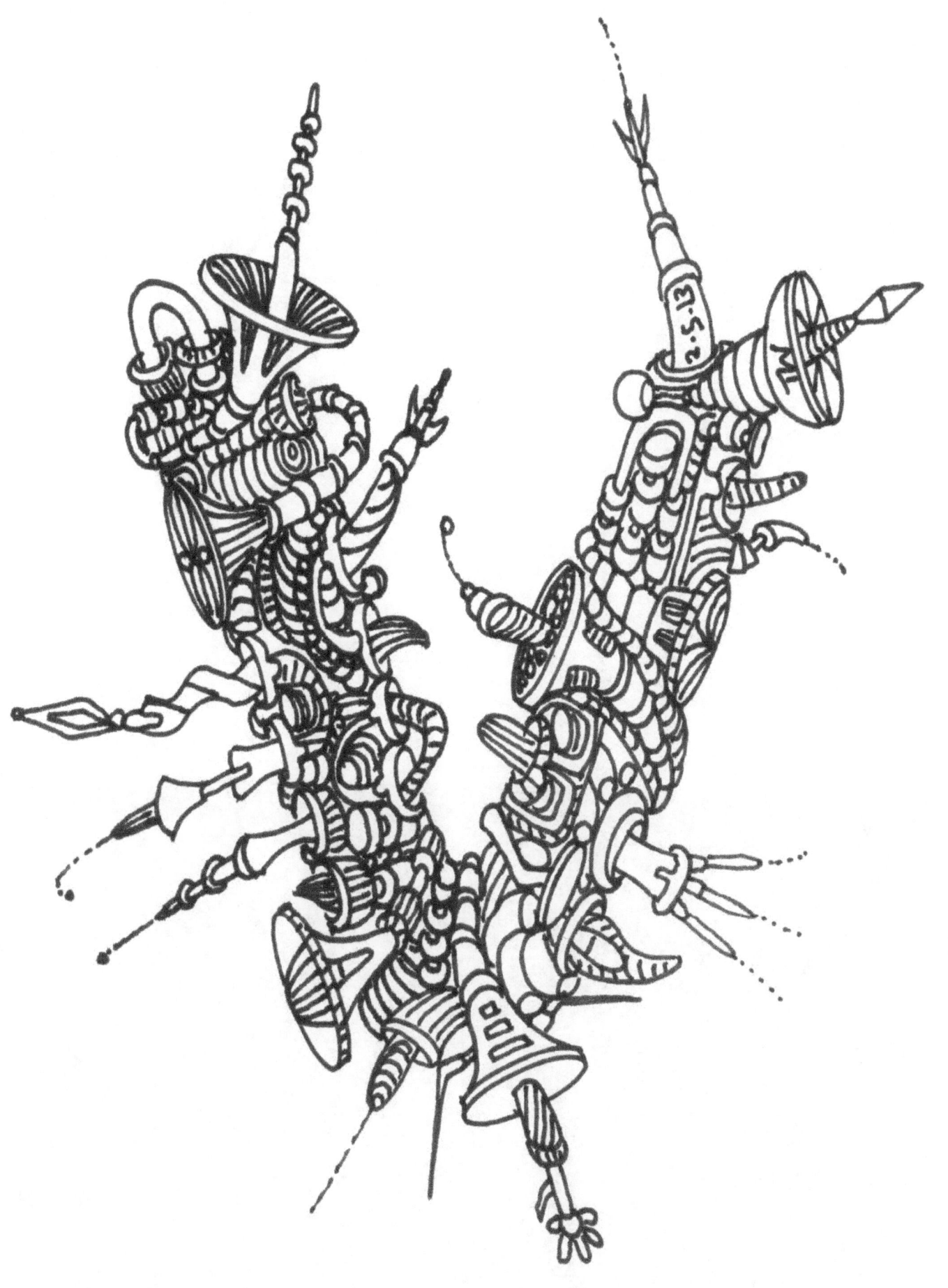

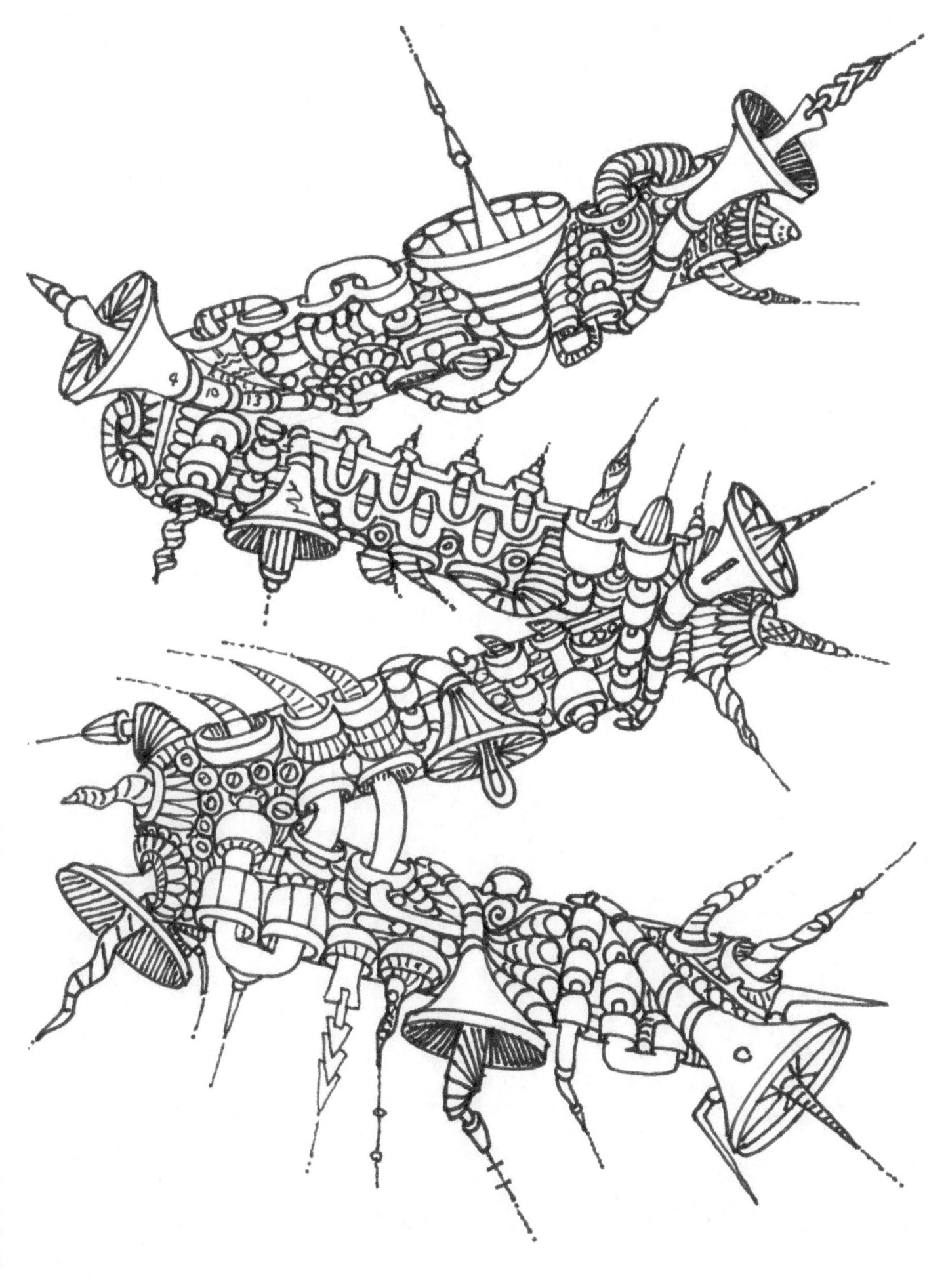

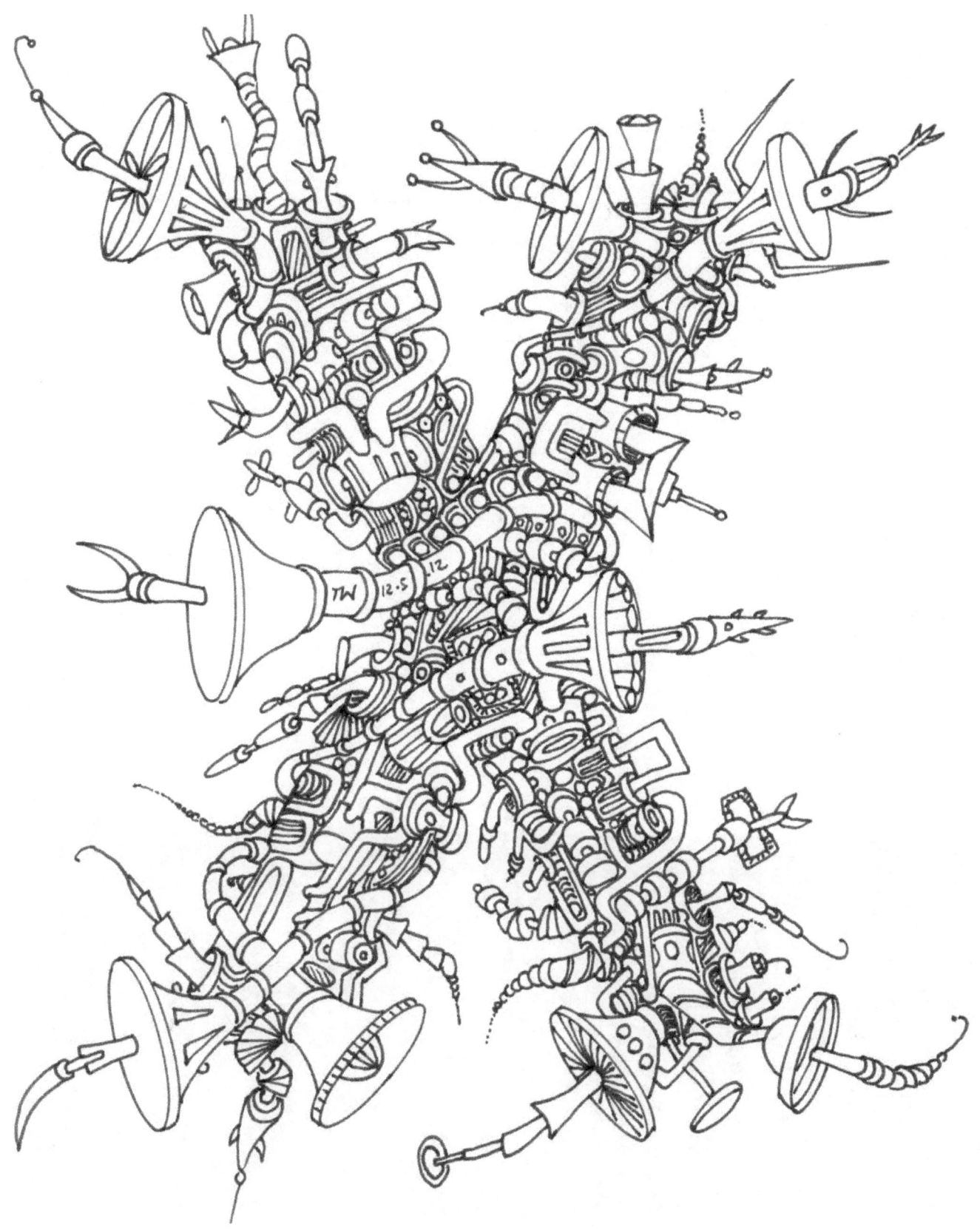

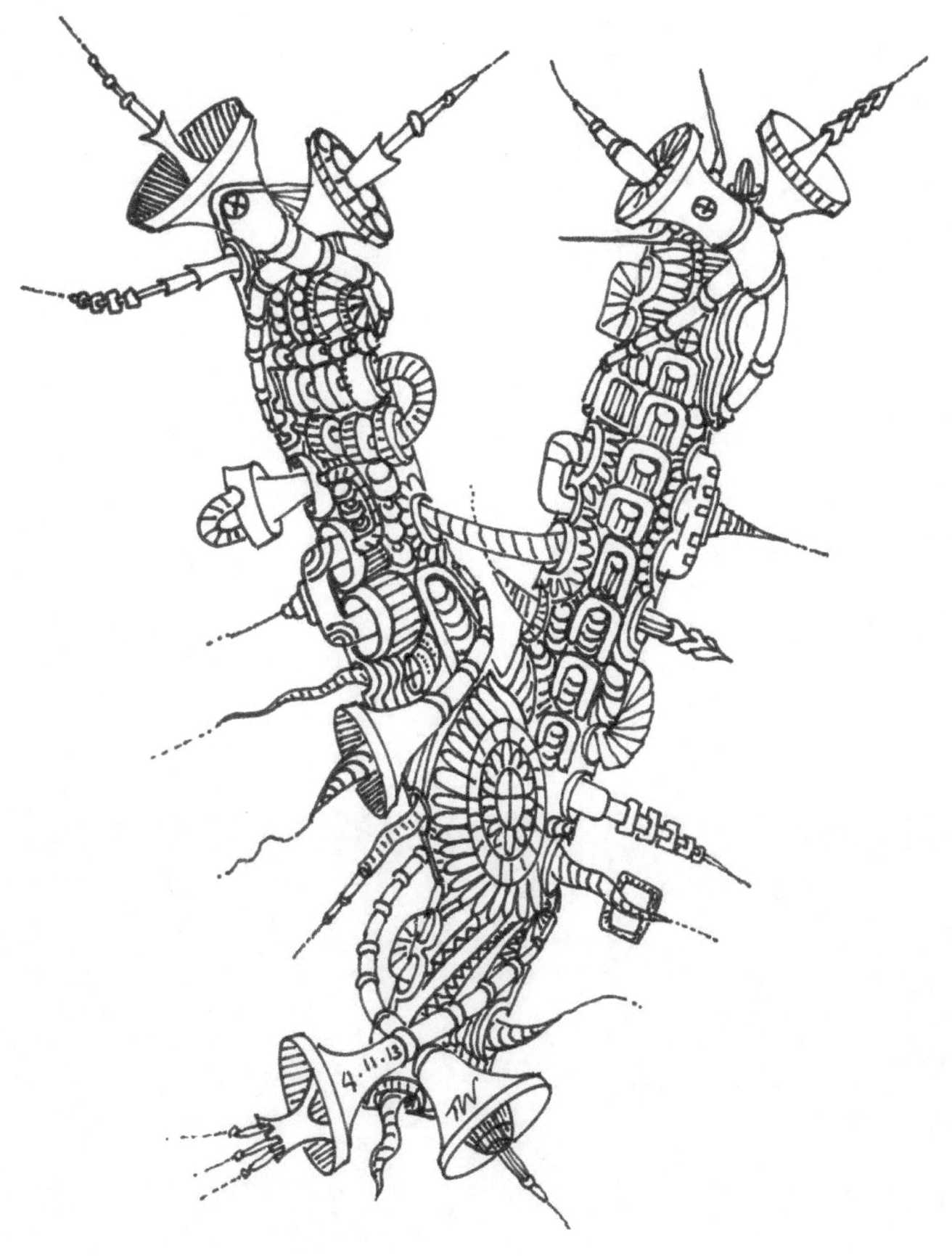

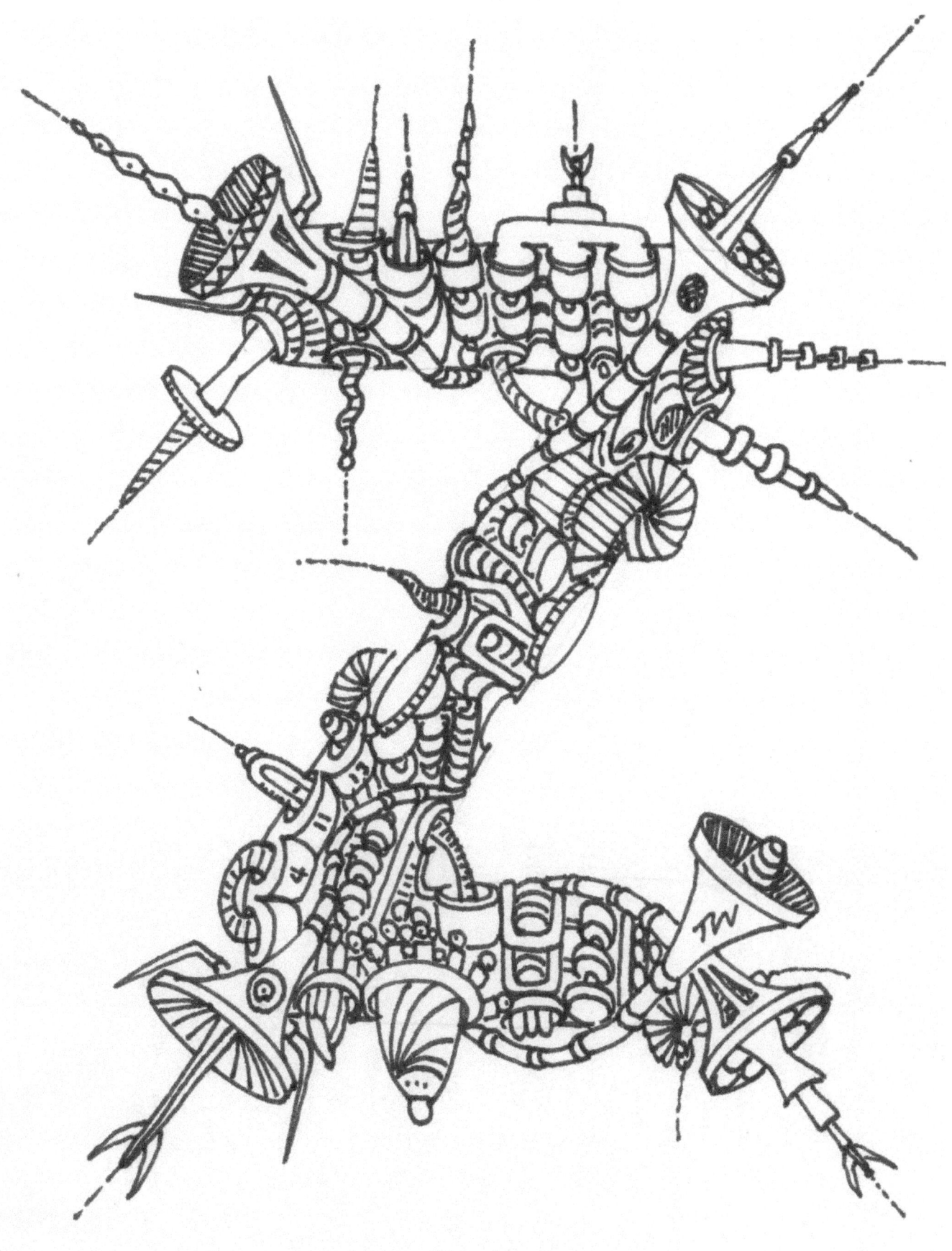